First World War
and Army of Occupation
War Diary
France, Belgium and Germany

38 DIVISION
Divisional Troops
176 Machine Gun Company
19 March 1917 - 28 February 1918

WO95/2548/4

The Naval & Military Press Ltd
www.nmarchive.com
Published in association with The National Archives

Published by

The Naval & Military Press Ltd

Unit 10 Ridgewood Industrial Park,

Uckfield, East Sussex,

TN22 5QE England

Tel: +44 (0) 1825 749494

www.naval-military-press.com

www.nmarchive.com

This diary has been reprinted in facsimile from the original. Any imperfections are inevitably reproduced and the quality may fall short of modern type and cartographic standards.

© Crown Copyright
Images reproduced by permission of The National Archives, London, England, 2015.

Contents

Document type	Place/Title	Date From	Date To
Heading	WO95/2548/4		
Heading	38th Division 176th Machine Gun Coy. Mar 1917-1918 Feb		
War Diary	Southampton	19/03/1917	19/03/1917
War Diary	Havre	20/03/1917	26/03/1917
War Diary	Poperinghe	28/03/1917	28/03/1917
War Diary	Elverdinghe	03/04/1917	24/04/1917
Heading	War Diary Of 176th Machine Gun Company From May 1st 1917 To June 4th 1917 (Volume 1)		
War Diary	Elverdinghe	01/05/1917	09/05/1917
War Diary	Boesinghe	10/05/1917	18/05/1917
War Diary	Vox Vrie "L" Line	19/05/1917	30/05/1917
War Diary	Vox Vrie	31/05/1917	04/06/1917
Heading	War Diary Of No. 176 Machine Gun Compy From 5-6-1917 To 30-6-1917 (Volume 4)		
War Diary	Elverdinghe & L' Line	05/06/1917	10/06/1917
War Diary	Elverdinghe & A10d11	09/06/1917	11/06/1917
War Diary	L Line & Vox Vrie Wood	12/06/1917	30/06/1917
Heading	War Diary Of The 176th M.G. Company From July 1st 1917 To August 6th 1917 Vol 5		
War Diary	Fontes	01/07/1917	04/07/1917
War Diary	Liettres	05/07/1917	11/07/1917
War Diary	Fontes	11/07/1917	14/07/1917
War Diary	Houleron	16/07/1917	16/07/1917
War Diary	Eecke	17/07/1917	18/07/1917
War Diary	Proven	19/07/1917	20/07/1917
War Diary	Voxvrie	20/07/1917	31/07/1917
War Diary	Pilrem	31/07/1917	06/08/1917
Operation(al) Order(s)	176 M.G. Coy. Operation Order No. 8	21/07/1917	21/07/1917
Miscellaneous	Machine Gun Fire Organisation O.O.8		
Operation(al) Order(s)	176 M G Company O.O. No 8 Addendum No 3	30/07/1917	30/07/1917
Operation(al) Order(s)	176 M.G. Coy Operation Order No 8 Addendum No 1	26/07/1917	26/07/1917
Operation(al) Order(s)	176 M.G. Coy. O.O. No. 8 Addendum No 2	29/07/1917	29/07/1917
Map	Map Showing Group Positions Barrages X S.O.S. Lines For M.G. Fire		
Heading	War Diary Of The 176 M.G. Company From Aug 1st 1917 To August 31 1917 Vol.6		
War Diary	Pilkem	01/08/1917	31/08/1917
Heading	War Diary Of The 176th Machine Gun Company From 1-9-1917 To 30.9.1917. Vol 7		
War Diary		01/09/1917	11/09/1917
War Diary	Eecke	12/09/1917	12/09/1917
War Diary	Morbecque	13/09/1917	14/09/1917
War Diary	Estaires	15/09/1917	15/09/1917
War Diary	Rabot Farm	16/09/1917	16/09/1917
War Diary	Armentieres	17/09/1917	30/09/1917
Heading	War Diary Of The 176th Machine Gun Company From 1.10.17 To 31.10.17. (Vol No 8)		
War Diary	Armentieres	01/10/1917	31/10/1917

Heading	War Diary Of The 176 Machine Gun Compy From 1-11-1917 To 30.11.1917 (Vol 9)		
War Diary	Armentieres	01/11/1917	30/11/1917
Heading	War Diary Of The 176th Machine Gun Company 1.12.1917 To 31.12.17 Vol 10		
War Diary	Armentieres	01/12/1917	18/12/1917
War Diary	Fort Rompu & Fleurbaix	19/12/1917	31/12/1917
Heading	War Diary Of The 176th Machine Gun Compy From 1.1.1918 To 31.1.1918 Vol 11		
War Diary	Fleurbaix	01/01/1918	15/01/1918
War Diary	Estaires	16/01/1918	19/01/1918
War Diary	Estaires	17/01/1918	31/01/1918
Heading	War Diary Of 176th Machine Gun Compy From 1.2.1918 To 28.2.1918 Vol 12		
War Diary	Guarbecque	01/02/1918	01/02/1918
War Diary	Enguinegatte	02/02/1918	11/02/1918
War Diary	Guarbecque	12/02/1918	12/02/1918
War Diary	La Gorgue Area	13/02/1918	13/02/1918
War Diary	Armentieres	14/02/1918	28/02/1918

Woods 125481/4

38TH DIVISION

176TH MACHINE GUN COY.

MAR 1917-~~MAR 1919~~ 1918 FEB

38TH DIVISION

Army Form C. 2118.

WAR DIARY
or
INTELLIGENCE SUMMARY
(Erase heading not required.)

176 Company E. Corps

Place	Date	Hour	Summary of Events and Information	Remarks and references to Appendices
Southampton	19/3/17	11 pm	Embarked for France.	
Havre	20/3/17	12.30 pm	Disembarked.	
"			From 20th to 26th remained in Rest Camp at Havre.	
"	26/3/17	1.30 pm	Entrained to join our Division in the Peronne area.	
Peronne	28/3/17	6.30 am	Detrained at Peronne & joined Division and went into billets in Peronne with the 31st Div.	

K.T. Thornam Lieut
O.C. 176 Coy

Army Form C. 2118.

WAR DIARY
or
INTELLIGENCE SUMMARY

(Erase heading not required.)

176 Machine Gun Company   Vol 2

Place	Date	Hour	Summary of Events and Information	Remarks and references to Appendices
ELVERDINGHE	April 3rd	3 pm	Nos 2 & 4 Section relieve Nos 1 & 3 Section who were in turn north 113 M.G. Coy.	
	6th	4.15 PM	after relief, No 1 & 3 Section took up position in 'L' lines defences, less ten 1 gun of No 1 Section. remained at H.Q. Coy. Von Vrie Camp	
	7th	2 pm	1 gun of No 1 Section at Coy. H.Q. rested up to 'L' line defence.	
	13th	4 pm	Nos 2 & 4 Section to the hors north. 113 M.S. Coy. returned to Coy H.Q.	
	17th	11 am	Nos 2 & 4 Section reduced Nos 1 & 3 Section in 'L' line defence.	
	24th	4 pm	Officers and N.C.O's inspected the VIII Corps School	
			Nos 1 & 3 Sections relieve Nos 2 & 4 Section in the 'L line defence.	

B Browne Clark

Vol 3

Confidential

War Diary
of

176th Machine Gun Company

From May 1st 1917 To June 4th 1917

(Volume 1)

WAR DIARY
or
INTELLIGENCE SUMMARY

Army Form C. 2118.

Place	Date	Hour	Summary of Events and Information	Remarks and references to Appendices
ELVERDINGHE	MAY 1st		We relieved the 113th M.G. Coy in the BOESINGHE SECTOR. This is the extreme Left sector of the British Line. On our left we had BELGIUM ARMY & on our right the 113th Infy Brigade. The relief was begun as soon as we had finished taking over the ELVERDINGHE & "Z" LINE Defences. By 4 pm the relief in the Ladder Line was complete & by 8.30 pm all reliefs had been effected. From that time we remained attached to the 114th Infy Brigade.	Bs.
	2nd		A reconnaissance of the sector was made by the C.O. & the following characteristics were noted. The French system to strongly simply there being any three communication trenches. There are three lines of defence — A Line, S Line & X Line. A line runs along the side of the YSER Canal, the canal being No Mans-Land. S Line is the main line of support, line & X Line being the second line of defence. The general scheme of defence was far as the Machine Guns were concerned was to defend the canal from S & X Lines with one exception. On [?] was also in "A" Line in such a position as to enfilade the enemy's front line at the point where it turned NORTH from the canal. The firm was not to open fire until the enemy attempted to cross to our further NORTH of the canal.	

WAR DIARY
or
INTELLIGENCE SUMMARY

Army Form C. 2118.

Place	Date	Hour	Summary of Events and Information	Remarks and references to Appendices
ELVERDINGHE	MAY 3rd 4th		Improvements to the positions occupied our attention during the day. A reconnaissance of all positions occupied was carried out by C.O. The attitude of the enemy was very unexpectant. No attempts whatsoever was made to snipe. It was quite safe to proceed anywhere in the open about 200 yards from the front line.	
	5th		Bay. O. Major of the 114th Brigade inspected the positions in "A" Line. Not heavy work.	
	6th		An intersection relief took place. The Locations of the Sections is as follows. N°1 Section "S" Line N°2 "SVA" line N°3 X Line N°4 Coy HQ ELVERDINGHE was heavily shelled early in the morning. Damage unknown.	
	7th		The enemy heavily shelled ELVERDINGHE during the early hours of the morning. H.Q. Section were forced to evacuate billets. The night was spent in a neighbouring hedge. Found street which was strewed but luckily evacuation avoided any casualties. The rear enemy of in the bombardment appears to rest, probably brought up night if is noticed that day bomb attacks them. Either none a quiet day.	
	8th		Weather was again very fine. The day was very quiet. As neglect relaxed on the activity of the enemys artillery on the two previous nights the Cops artillery carried out a programme of fire on the enemys line recommenced in at 8.30 p.m. again at 11 striking slight casualties from death ensured. A quiet day. No enemy artillery casualties	
	9th			

to Pte Hastings R.N. & Section

War Diary or Intelligence Summary

Army Form C. 2118.

Place	Date	Hour	Summary of Events and Information	Remarks and references to Appendices
BOESINGHE	May 10		C.O. inspected all positions. Enemy often active during the forenoon. Artillery was fairly active during the forenoon. Section 1 in A line. An inter-section relief took place. Expiration of duties Section No 2 in reserve. Section 3 in S line. Section 4 in X line.	
	11th		An uneventful day.	
	12th		New site for Cpl M.G. commenced to wired at B.17.a.32. Hostile artillery was fairly active during the forenoon doing some damage to communication trenches. Sgt E. McLester taken in the strength & posted as sub. section sergt to section 3.	
	13th		Fair weather continued. The only event of the day worth mentioning was a successful attack on a Belgian Balloon by the enemy. My mg gun crews, damaged whilst endeavouring not withstanding our troops and shell damage, whilst empty its pursuers to the vicinity of the Balloon, passing over a minute or so the Balloon burst into flames & was lapped out before it could be landed. Successful parachute descent was made by the observer. Drivel to Ypres SAFE again after a spell of 14 days DANGEROUS A 4 hours army. Nothing to report.	
	14th			
	15th		An information relief took place. Inspection to Sections: A line No 3 Section. "S" line No 4 Section. X line No 2 Section. W9s No 1 Section.	
	16th		Hot weather. Against army.	
	17th		The Brigade was relieved by the 115th M.G.Coy. on relief we withdrew 114 M.G.Coy in L'Vecu afferding inspection after relief Section 1st in L'Cine Marthoma 2nd & 3rd at Nee Ecure	
	18th			

Army Form C. 2118.

WAR DIARY
or
INTELLIGENCE SUMMARY
(Erase heading not required.)

Instructions regarding War Diaries and Intelligence Summaries are contained in F. S. Regs., Part II. and the Staff Manual respectively. Title Pages will be prepared in manuscript.

Place	Date	Hour	Summary of Events and Information	Remarks and references to Appendices
Not known "L" Lines	May 19th		The day was spent in sorting out equipment. A gun team was engaged in battle. continued the Contest	Sent to Reports 20th March
	20th		Sunday – a quiet day on the farm.	
	21st		A programme of training was commenced. Weather cloudy.	
	22nd		Hot weather. Training continued. Several recruits from a large gun were put into Reserve.	
	23rd		Very Good and very exercises were carried out.	
	24th		Section 2 & 3 received tuition & arts inspection in L" Line. Horse Camp is now pending the occupation by no the B fox out Camp. This camp is now approved up that would be camp offices and work on it by this end. Fine weather continued.	
	25th		This day was spent in preparing for target firing & a programme of training was carried out.	
	26th		Telephone to & Line situation and an Inspect.	
	27th		Sunday. Church parade took place as after parade.	
	28th		A tactical scheme was run. Orders was carried out by section officers.	
	29th		A working party of two occupied in the construction of transport lines near the after G on new camp at A.10.d.11. Equipment for camps and harness for ran brought to the employment in & Line Station.	
	30			

Army Form C. 2118.

WAR DIARY
or
INTELLIGENCE SUMMARY
(Erase heading not required.)

Place	Date	Hour	Summary of Events and Information	Remarks and references to Appendices
Vot Brie	May 31st June 1st		Right firing of munitions commenced.	
	2nd		No firing took place owing to our working parties	
	3rd		My to firing continued	
	4th		do	
			do.	

Vol 4

Confidential

War Diary

of

No. 176 Machine Gun Compy

From 5.6.1917 to 30.6.1917

(Volume)

WAR DIARY
or
INTELLIGENCE SUMMARY

(Erase heading not required.)

Army Form C. 2118.

Place	Date	Hour	Summary of Events and Information	Remarks and references to Appendices
EVERDINGHE "L" LINE	June 5th		The enemy have shown greatly increased activity in shelling back areas. This activity appears to be increasing daily. He continued the nightly firing. Roads + communication trenches were shelled intermittently throughout the night causing much disorganisation + delay. Intelligence reports that recent bombardments by our artillery have caused much damage, resulting in the exposure of many concrete dugouts. A hostile aeroplane dropped three bombs on 10x VIII Camp causing no damage.	
	6th/7th		Nightly firing was increased by the addition of the 8 guns on "L" Line. Before Zero time was fixed for 3.10 a.m. Owing to unfavourable wind gas masks were not attended as intended. Hostile artillery has been very active on all communications. Operations by Ohio Comy (2nd) are stated to be progressing satisfactorily.	
	8th		Gas projections were sent over at 2.30 a.m. he carried run harassing fire from X Lim Stevain. Owing to neglect of a Macdoning MG Order a fatal accident occurred to Pte A.E. Swan. This man Macdodin [?] on the gun + he went infront of the Cross-head before [?] unloading to adjust to the fire screen. The [?] was intensely black. Another man approached told him that No 1 was to fire J the gun, fired the gun nearly to the head crust [?] the brass [?] of the Loans.	
	9th to 10th		He carried out an area shoot on same targets with nightly firing. Guns were switched from one target to another welcomed[?] fire was brought to bear. Gun was employed that a relay was taking place in the Broewing[?] Shelter. It is possible that a success and result to humanleads[?] after 3.0 a.m. when the Shelling	AG

2449 Wt. W14957/M90 750,000 1/16 J.B.C. & A. Forms/C.2118/12.

WAR DIARY
or
INTELLIGENCE SUMMARY
(Erase heading not required.)

Army Form C. 2118.

Place	Date	Hour	Summary of Events and Information	Remarks and references to Appendices
FEVERDINGHE + A.od 11	June 1917 9th & 10th		sounded for day then continued the enemy standing well back field from in a very broad manner search gun emplacement & our loops. About 100 rounds were fired. 91 — suggests that this was retaliation to our fire. Recently our gun have had a clean career. Perhaps which unfortunately occur to the new muzzle-cap. Three accidents have occurred when the front some has been blown out of the muzzle attachment. 91 in suggests that the cause of this is the new muzzle-cup which does not allow sufficient space for the gases to escape after rebounding with muzzle cup. The result is that the front open returned on to the barrel core causing (to be ripped) out together filth and there after term.	
		11ʰ	A violent bombardment broke out at 10.30 pm (10ᵗʰ). It has not ceased to-day. The day was spent in overhauling guns material. Our recent night firing expended 50,000 rounds short of half a million round. Our chief breakages were undoubtedly lock springs which appear to be unable to stand the strain. Gibbs springs & firing pins caused some trouble. No muzzle cups were broken but Ed. attachment suffered as mentioned under date of the 10ᵗʰ inst.	

WAR DIARY or INTELLIGENCE SUMMARY

Army Form C. 2118.

Place	Date	Hour	Summary of Events and Information	Remarks and references to Appendices
"L" LINE & VOORMEZEELE WOOD	June 12		Training was recommenced. Construction of Cook House & the erecting of an extra well was begun. Work is becoming a difficult problem & I have received orders to again send our camp. This necessitates the evacuation of our newly completed office, stable, surgeon, etc. The men occupied us all day. Weather still very hot. Bugs & vermin a very great problem.	Map May Belgium 28 N.W. / Vesour
	13			
	14/15			
	16		Section 203 relieved below I.M. in "L" line. The construction of shelters from shelling was commenced. From these positions it is possible to fire overhead covering fire. The emplacements approximately one rifleman will a firm rule 7 pm. he has one man severely wounded while on a carrying party.	
	17		Four overhead emplacements were completed.	
	18		Hostile artillery has shown greatly increased activity both in forward & back areas. Trenches nearby to preparing new continued.	
	19		Training continued. We have had 21 men attacked from the infantry. The present establishment has again been found to be inadequate owing to additional duties of mounting guard for casemate wagons.	

2449 Wt. W14957/Mg0 750,000 1/16 J.B.C. & A. Forms/C.2118/12.

WAR DIARY
or
INTELLIGENCE SUMMARY

Army Form C. 2118.

Place	Date	Hour	Summary of Events and Information	Remarks and references to Appendices
A Line VOX VRIE WOOD	Aug 20		The attack on personnel continued their training as heretofore. Two 9 guns were moved up for the protection of dumps. Hostile aeroplanes have shown a little more daring recently than is their wont but it is always driven the early reconnaissance when they came over at dawn — at our aerodrome. The early morning visit so incredibly anxiously awaited by the previous day's dropping of bombs which so slightly damage to the camps.	
	21st		Weather today is cooler — however his clumps, they spent the day in sleepy movement have closed the air. Today a slight wind has risen. The shelling of back areas was again the object of hostile artillery. A direct hit was obtained on the C.O.'s tent with a 5.9 HV. The effect was entirely confined to a radius of 7 yards about the point of entry. No casualties occurred although there were about 30 persons within 15 yards one man being within 2 yards. These shells appear to have such such a velocity that they penetrate to a considerable depth before detonating with the result that all energy is taken up in raising the ground no pieces appear to have reached the surface.	

WAR DIARY
or
INTELLIGENCE SUMMARY
(Erase heading not required.)

Army Form C. 2118.

Place	Date	Hour	Summary of Events and Information	Remarks and references to Appendices
"L" Line & 1st Line Sub-d.	June 22nd		Hostile H.V. guns & howitzers were very active in back area.	Map Ref Belgium 28 N.W. 1/20,000
	23rd		Rainfall heavy during the day. Weather very changeable. Training was continued. Hostile artillery was less active in back areas.	
	24		Fine weather favoured. At 3.20 a.m. a hostile plane was heavily engaged & appeared to be hit our M.G.s in ELVERDINGHE. Observers reported that they engaged a hostile plane in addition to A.A. Batteries & it was brought down in our lines. This was probably the same plane. During the night 10 detachment N.Q. ELVERDINGHE opened heavy shelled with H.V. gun. Three direct hits were obtained one officer being seriously wounded & two men.	
	25th		Few weather continued. About 8.30pm a hostile plane came during reconnaissance of our bivouac area flying at about 3000 feet. A fight took place that the was heavily engaged with A.A. Batteries, M.G.s & Lewis Guns. He managed to make good his escape with half an hour before he came in again on the area flown over with the result that the A.M.C. was badly hit killing men & horses. My Coy sub. returned on the release the horses stampeded in the direction of POPERINGHE Thro' returning with us rifle avalanche & fire. Air reconnaissance & communication	NC

WAR DIARY
or
INTELLIGENCE SUMMARY
(Erase heading not required.)

Army Form C. 2118.

Place	Date	Hour	Summary of Events and Information	Remarks and references to Appendices
"L" Line & VOXVRIE WOOD	Aug 26		Fine weather – quiet day. In "L" Line we had one man seriously wounded.	Map Ref BELGIUM 28 NW 1/20,000 HAZEBROUK 5A. 1/100,000
	27"		Rather cooler day. We sent two officers to billet in advance at CAESTRE & FONTES.	
	28"		We were relieved by the 88" M.G. Coy in "L" Line & the A.A. guns at VOXVRIE WOOD.	
	29"		Reveille 5.0.a.m. The personnel travelled to HONDEGHEM by bus, the transport proceeding by road. We arrived at 2.30 pm & the transport at 3.0 p.m. without casualty.	
	30"		We moved on 6 NORRENT FONTES & reoccupied same. The transport was parked & the men billeted in the open. Notwithstanding the fact that the transport has not trekked for 4 month the journey — about 30 miles in all — was accomplished without casualty.	

Confidential   Vol 5

War Diary

of the 176th M.G. Company

from July 1st 1917   to August 6th 1917

(Vol.   )

Army Form C. 2118.

WAR DIARY
or
INTELLIGENCE SUMMARY
(Erase heading not required.)

Instructions regarding War Diaries and Intelligence Summaries are contained in F. S. Regs., Part II. and the Staff Manual respectively. Title Pages will be prepared in manuscript.

Place	Date 1917	Hour	Summary of Events and Information	Remarks and references to Appendices
FONTES.	July 1		The day was spent in sorting equipment checking numbers. This is the first occasion it has had to house the equipment of the Company since the commencement of April.	MARRIED:— HAZEBROUCK 1/10,000
	2nd		Training commenced. Reveille 6.0 am 6.15–6.45 am P.T. 7.0 am Breakfast, 8.0 am I.O. inspection. 8.15–9.15 am continued drill using the New Manuals as laid down on Pgs. 79 I.M.G.C. Training Manual; 9.15–10.30 am Belt-filling by machine (hand Benifields) 11–12.30 pm Action from Pack Mules; 2.3.0 pm Barrage drill, saddling.	
	3rd		Training continued on lines indicated above.	
	4th		Tactical Scheme was carried out in the morning — taken from Pack Mules. The attacking party advancing had been ordered to go saddling.	
LIETTRES.	5th		We moved from FONTES to LIETTRES. Accommodation in this place as from Attached orders were carried out under S.O.'s.	
	6th		... with opening approach ...	
	7th		Raining most ...	
	8th		Quite settled the day	
	9th		...	
	10th		The ...	
	11th		...	

WAR DIARY
or
INTELLIGENCE SUMMARY

(Erase heading not required.)

Army Form C. 2118.

Place	Date	Hour	Summary of Events and Information	Remarks and references to Appendices
TONTES	11		Continued...	
	12			
	13		Jiu-jitsu & similar subjects were rubbed up during the day.	
	14		Arranged other events. A route march in Box Respirators for one hour was tried. Report on very satisfactory, & reported to covering point comfortable after a few minutes.	
	15		The Company tricked to HOULERON	
HOULERON	16		We moved to EECKE	
EECKE	17			
	18		We changed billets	
PROVEN	19		We marched to PROVEN.	
VOXVRIE	20		We relieved 4 AA guns near the camp of the 87 M.G.Cy. 600 were exchanged by inspection on the bivouacs at from 2.9.0 a.m. (21st inst)	
	21st			
	22		The day was spent in exchanging equipment.	
	23		A programme of revision of subjects was carried out	
	24		The day was spent in preparation for active operations to commence shortly.	

WAR DIARY
or
INTELLIGENCE SUMMARY
(Erase heading not required.)

Army Form C. 2118.

Place	Date	Hour	Summary of Events and Information	Remarks and references to Appendices
VOX VRIE	July 25		Operation Orders a copy of which is attached were issued.	Maps Ref Sheet 28 N.W. Ypres BELGIUM
	27 & 28		We prepared an assembly trench ready S.A.A. dumps. E.y.th. CANAL BANK. At noon we received orders to standby for attack. We remained on short notice throughout the day. It appears that the enemy have retired to the neighbourhood of Pilckem. MACKEM. but the situation is by no means clear. Our patrols cd. find no hold of our own further enemy's front line.	
	29/30		All material required for the operation were placed in the assembly trench under the care of a guard. Our artillery were distinctly more active than the enemy's.	
	30th		This "Y" day. At 9.30 p.m. the company less 2 runners of 24 gunners C.S.M., bodyguards, two corporals two officers, moved into the assembly trench on the Canal Bank. This was Zero day with Zero time at 3.50 a.m.	
	31st onward for 6 days		Our first position being behind the enemy's second line. The company cd. not move forward until 5.10 am. Our difficulties were at once seen with regard to keeping direction. Owing to the intensity of our artillery preparation few landmarks remained, whilst map was of little avail except to give a rough direction. The RIGHT GROUPS under 2/Lt HG Marshall M	

WAR DIARY
or
INTELLIGENCE SUMMARY

Army Form C. 2118.

Place	Date	Hour	Summary of Events and Information	Remarks and references to Appendices
PILKEM	July 31st	Aug 6	All guns were then laid for an S.O.S. call on the front of LANGEMARK village. By this time if was about 11·30 a.m. The first S.O.S. call came at 4.15 p.m. when a strong counter attack was launched. This was entirely broken up by our M.G. fire (Infantry report). Roughly estimating the number of balls per gun at that time would be about 8. At 11·0 a.m. the Transport Officer located the gun positions & by 3·0 p.m. had brought 18 mules with 36,000 rds of S.A.A. to a dump at IRON CROSS. By night fall the guns were well established & remained in their positions until 4·0 a.m. on August 6th when they were withdrawn with the rest of the Division who were relieved by the 20th (LIGHT) Dn. The weather was wretched during the first five days, & rain being practically continuous. This caused the greatest discomfort to the teams who were in the open in shell holes practically the whole of the six days. The approach to PILKEM became impossible even to pack animals & the supply	BIXSCHOOTE 1/40,000

WAR DIARY
or
INTELLIGENCE SUMMARY

Army Form C. 2118.

Place	Date	Hour	Summary of Events and Information	Remarks and references to Appendices
PILKEM	July 31/8 Aug 6.		Dumping of rations & ammunition was accomplished by carriers from a forward dump. This occupied the limit of approach for pack animals. The early arrival of the pack animals on Zero day was a great advance & was only accomplished by great determination on the part of the Transport Officer. During this period our guns answered about 16 S.O.S. calls & Several the infantry call. Our casualties were 3 officers wounded. 9 O.R. killed 27 O.R. wounded & 4 O.R. missing. Owing to the inadequate personnel of an M.G. Coy we had 56 infantry attached for purposes of carrying parties. They proved to be most unreliable for the following reasons:– 1. The all others personnel had not the work of the company at heart consequently much material was lost. 2. We were unable to recognize our carriers. A badge is absolutely necessary. 3. Unsuitable men were sent to us as carriers	Casualties:– 2/Lt Mitchell 2/Lt Hamilton 2/Lt Murphy

WAR DIARY or INTELLIGENCE SUMMARY

Army Form C. 2118.

Place	Date	Hour	Summary of Events and Information	Remarks and references to Appendices
PILKEM.	July 31st to Aug 6.		& 2nd Lt Fry Price 2nd Lt W.J. Murphy managed with great difficulty to reach their chosen position in accordance with the Operation Order attached. These groups managed to get SB & bells for guns by the appointed time for cease fire in the 1st position i.e. + 5.9. The LEFT GROUPS in the meantime were unable to find their first position, realizing the importance of the second position these groups under 2Lt J.O.Hamilton & 2Lt J.R. Hamilton pushed forward towards PILKEM. The C.O. Lt Col. Adamson after despatching the groups from the assembly trench to their 1st position pushed ahead & located the LEFT GROUPS in the 1st position, leaving them he went to the RIGTH GROUPS & joining them without sufficient time to shoot the 1st Barrage ordered them to proceed to the vicinity of IRON CROSS. The C.O. proceeded these groups & met the G.O.C. 116 Inf. Brig. at IRON CROSS in accordance with instructions. In the meantime our infantry has obtained this last objective & were established along the time of STEENBEEK. After an interview with the O.C. Left Battalion it was decided to bring the groups into action along the road running SE from IRONCROSS.	BIXSCHOOTE Order No. 300

2449 Wt. W14957/M90 750,000 1/16 J.B.C. & A. Forms/C.2118/12.

Army Form C. 2118.

WAR DIARY
or
INTELLIGENCE SUMMARY
(Erase heading not required.)

Instructions regarding War Diaries and Intelligence Summaries are contained in F.S. Regs., Part II. and the Staff Manual respectively. Title Pages will be prepared in manuscript.

Place	Date	Hour	Summary of Events and Information	Remarks and references to Appendices
PILKEM	July 31st	Aug 6	Reference objects were unobtainable in the firing position. The auxiliary aiming mark mentioned in the operation order Aerodrome No 2 could not be seen from the first position. It is highly improbable that any R.O. can be found immediately after an attack in which push + gas are used, owing to the small field of vision.	

R.H. Alcocer Capt.
Comdg. 176 M.G.C.

SECRET.   176 M.G. Coy.
              Operation Order No. 8
                                              21.7.1917

Ref. Maps 1/10,000 St. Julien 28 N.W. 2 Edition 5A.
                    Bixschook 20 S.W.

Plan   The 176 M.G. Coy will operate in the attack
of the 38th Division on "Z" Day at Zero
hour, both of which will be notified
later.
       The attack will be made in a series of
bounds as defined on the attached map.

       1st Bound — BLUE LINE
       2nd Bound — BLACK LINE
       3rd Bound — GREEN LINE
       4th Bound — GREEN DOTTED LINE.

       Beyond the GREEN DOTTED LINE, the Cavalry
will ascertain if the enemy are holding
LANGEMARCK in strength.

Distribution   The 114 Infty. Brigade will attack on the
of   RIGHT and the 113 Infty. Brigade will attack
Infantry   on the LEFT. The 115 Infty. Brigade will be in
reserve & will move forward & take over any
ground held by the Cavalry.

Strong Point All objectives will be consolidated &
particular attention will be paid to :-

       BLUE LINE :-   By 114 Infty. Brigade
                      GALLWITZ FARM ENCLOSURE at C 8 d 08.
                      By 113 Infty. Brigade
                      HOUSE 10 ZOUAVE HOUSE.

       BLACK LINE :- By 114 Infty Brigade
                      JOLIE FARM ENCLOSURE, the centre of which
                      is at C 2 d.30.02.
                      By 113 Infty. Brigade
                      ENCLOSURE near P. of PILKEM.
                      TELEGRAPH HOUSE.

GREEN LINE:— By 114th Infty. Brigade
ENCLOSURE at C4 a 05.45
ENCLOSURE from C3 b 45.70
to U 27 d 25.20
ABOUT C 3 b 25.30
By 113 Infty. Brigade
ENCLOSURE, of which centre is

U. 27 c 50. 34
U 27 c 65. 73
U 27 c 90. 33.

LINE OF STEENBEEK. The 115 Infty. Brigade will make Bridgeheads at AU BON GITE, U 28 a 30.55 and U 28 a 10.80.

RED LINE & LANGEMARCK. As the cavalry advances the 115 Infty. Brigade will hold the main lines.
(i) Western edge of LANGEMARCK
(ii) 300 yards N.E. of LANGEMARCK
(iii) RED LINE.

MACHINE GUNS

The 176 M.G. Coy. will, with two other M.G. Coys. form the Corps & Divisional Barrages.

The Barrage is directed so as to fall 500 yards beyond the Artillery creeping Barrages.

The attached Maps 3. 3A, 3B. show the M.G. Barrages.

The guns are divided into three main groups, two groups maintaining fire while the remaining group advances.

Apart from forming a creeping barrage, groups are so sited that they can fire an "S.O.S" barrage in front of each objective.

The 176 M.G. Coy. will be groups O.P.Q.R & O.O.,P.P., Q.Q. & R.R., The second groups O.O. P.P. Q.Q. R.R. are not shown on the map as their position depends on the

The "S.O.S" line (O2. P2. Q2. R2.) is to be maintained on the EAST BANK of the STEENBEEK.

The C.O. will arrange further barrages as required by the 115 Infty Brigade.

Two runners will be kept at the nearest exchange to receive messages.

When Coy. H.Q. move forward the D.M.G.O will be advised of its new location also the number of rounds fired from the first position.

TARGETS & RATE OF FIRE
Targets & rates of fire are shown on the attached forms.

"S.O.S" CALL

The "S.O.S" call will be fired by rifle grenades which will burst into
Two REDS
&
Two GREEN LIGHTS.

Dumps.
Ammunition & Water Dumps will be created for Z. day, places will be made known later.

Reserve Personnel

2 Sergeants, 2 Corporals & a reserve 24 gun numbers will be left behind at the Transport lines.

Transport
The Transport will move on "Y" night & be located about B20a74 (Sheet 28 N.W.)

Surplus kit & Baggage
All surplus kit & baggage will be dump at the present camp A16a88.

25/7/17

A.H. Adams Lt.
Cmdg. 176 M.G.C.

Machine Gun Fire Organisation. O.O.8.

No. of Group or Bty	No. of Guns	Composition	Commander	Location	Firing From Zero	Firing To Zero	Target	Rate of Fire	Remarks
O	4	Section 3	2/Lt H.C. Marshall	C.8.b.54.55	+3.20 +3.45		① C.4.a.52.59 To C.4.a.23.81	250 rds. per 3 min per gun	This is also S.O.S. Target. Rate of fire will be as in footnote on signal.
					+3.47 +5.9		② U.28.d.62.45 To U.28.d.41.78	50 rds per min per gun	
O.O.	"	"	"	Unknown	+5.9		Depends on situation		
P	4	" 2	2/Lt Ledbetter	C.8.b.46.67	+3.20 +3.45		① C.4.a.2381 To U.27.d.90.32	as above	do.
					+3.47 +5.9		② U.28.d.40.82 To U.28.b.0517	do	
P.P.	"	"	"	Unknown	5.9		Depends on situation		
Q	4	" 1	2/Lt W. Hamilton	C.8.b.3065	+3.20 +3.45		① U.27.d.54.35 To U.27.d.28.64	as above	do.
					+3.47 +5.5		② U.28.a.85.00 To U.28.a.62.30	do	
Q.Q.	"	"	"	Unknown	+5.5		Depends on situation	do	
R	4	" 4	2/Lt G.R. Hamilton	C.8.a.22.78	+3.20 +3.45		① U.27.d.2764 To U.27.c.97.95	250 rds per 3 min per gun	do.
					+3.47 +5.5		② U.28.a.4244 To U.28.a.0570		
R.R.	"	"	"	Unknown	5.5		Depends on situation	50 rds per min per gun	

On "S.O.S." rapid for 1st ten minutes then 2000 rounds per hour per gun.

2000 rounds in belts must always be kept with each gun to answer "S.O.S." call.

"S.O.S." call seeing that the enemy's infantry is commencing attacking will be coloured Rifle Grenade burst into TWO REDS & TWO GREEN LIGHTS.

If a gun becomes a casualty the remainder will extend their harness engaging the whole length as before.

176 M G Company O O No 8
addendum No 3

Times

Zero Day will be the 31st of July 1917
Zero Time will be 3.50 am on that day.
Teams will leave the concentration trench at 5.10 am
& will commence to fire 1st shoot at 7.10 am
                                  2nd shoot at 7.37 am
Cease fire in first position at 8.55 am & 8.59 am respectively for left & right groups.

30/7/17

Williamson Lt
for O.C. 176 M.G. Cy

SECRET

<u>176. M.G. Coy</u>
<u>Operation Order No 8</u>
<u>Addendum No 1</u>

<u>Calculations</u>

In making calculations at least three possible R.O.s should be taken & the deviation known.

A copy of calculations will be given to each gun number & an exchange made between S. Officers who will be working in their vicinity on Z day.

Copies of calculations on NCOs & men will carried in the top right hand tunic pocket.

S.Os will train two intelligent N.C.O's before X day so that they will be able once in position to lay the guns in case of need.

26/9/17

B. Williamson
Lt
for O.C. 176 M.G. Coy

176 M.G. Coy. O.O No.8
Addendum No 2

AUXILIARY AIMING POST

An auxiliary aiming post, 30 feet in height, painted black with a white triangle with a red border has been erected at C.19.a.62.82 by the Topographical Section.

Calculations will be amended & show this as one of the R.O's for possible use.

LOCATION OF COMPY. H.Q.

Compy. H.Q. from midnight 30/31st to Zero + 1.30 will be at C19.a.41 & after that time it will move forward to the vicinity of GALLWITZ FARM.

29/7/17

R. Williamson Lt
for OC 176 MG Coy

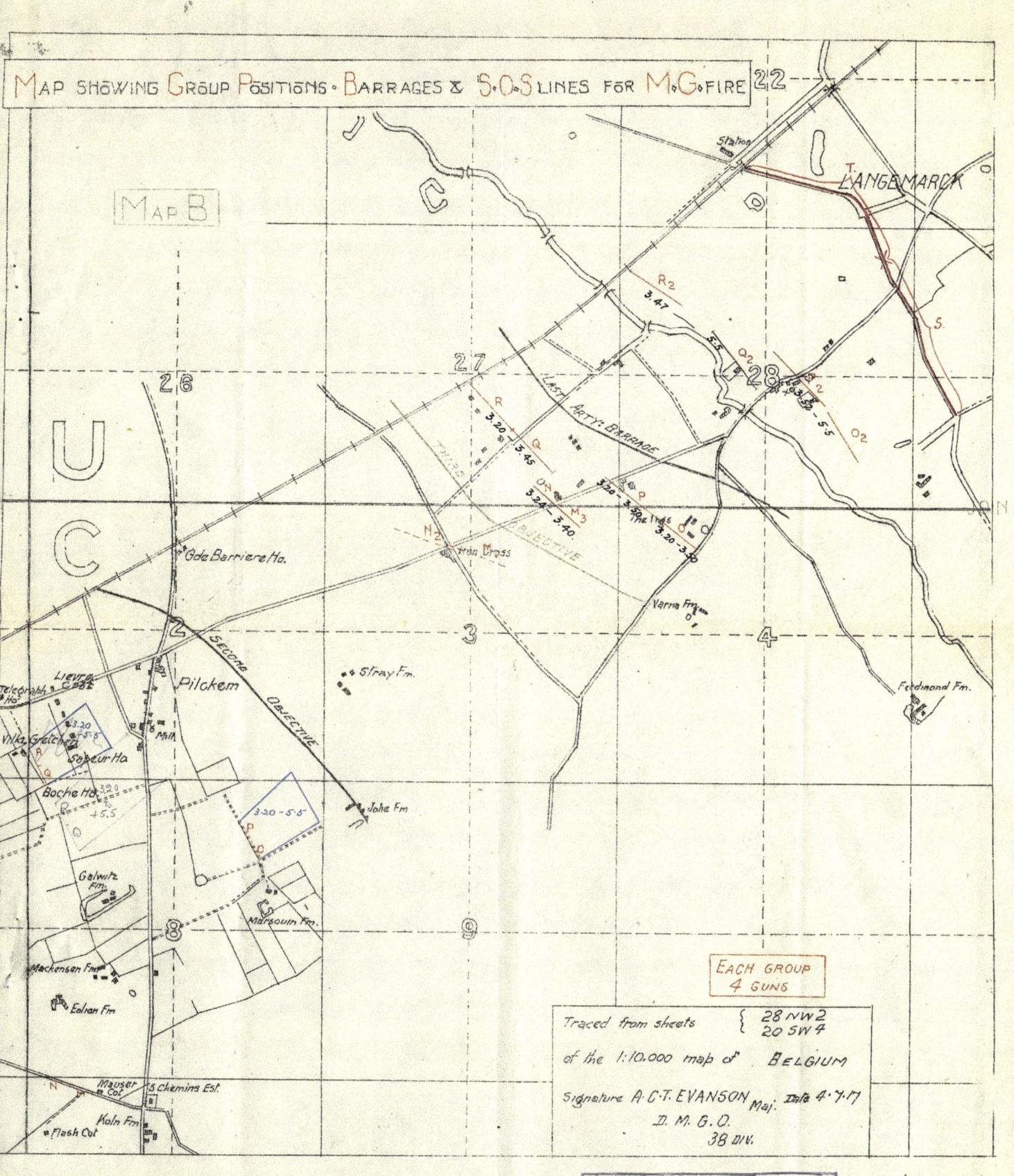

Vol 6

Confidential

War Diary

of the 176 M.G. Company

from Aug 1st 1917 to August 31st 1917

(Vol.)

WAR DIARY
or
INTELLIGENCE SUMMARY

(Erase heading not required.)

Army Form C. 2118.

Place	Date	Hour	Summary of Events and Information	Remarks and references to Appendices
PILKEM.	August 1st to 6th		We remained in these positions until 4 a.m. 6th. We were then withdrawn with the rest of the Division, who were being relieved by the 20th (Right) Division. The weather was wretched during the first five days, rain being practically continuous. This caused the greatest discomfort to the gun teams who were in shell holes, practically the whole of six days. The approach to PILKEM became impossible even to pack animals, even the supply of rations & ammunition was accomplished by carrier from a forward dump. This dump being the limit of approach for pack animals. The early arrival of pack animals on 2nd day was a great advantage, & was only accomplished by great determination on the part of the Transport Officer. During this period our guns answered about 16 S.O.S. calls & saved the infantry well. Our casualties were 3 Officers wounded & 9 O.R. killed, 27 O.R. wounded & 2 O.R. missing. Owing to inadequate personnel of a M.G. Company we lent 56 Infantry earmarked for purpose of carrying parties. They proved to be most unreliable, for the following reasons: 1. The attached personnel had not the workings of the Company at heart, & consequently much material was lost. 2. We were unable to recognise our carriers. A breakage in distinctly necessary. 3. Unsuitable men were sent to us as carriers. Reference depots were unobtainable in the first position. The Auxiliary Aiming Mark mentioned in attached Operation Order Oddendum No 2 could not be seen from the first position. It is highly important that any suitable R.O. can be found immediately after an attack in which guns & mortars are used owing to the unusual field of vision.	BIXSCHOOTE 1/10,000

Army Form C. 2118.

WAR DIARY
or
INTELLIGENCE SUMMARY
(Erase heading not required.)

Instructions regarding War Diaries and Intelligence Summaries are contained in F. S. Regs., Part II. and the Staff Manual respectively. Title Pages will be prepared in manuscript.

Place	Date	Hour	Summary of Events and Information	Remarks and references to Appendices
PILKEM	August 7th		The day was spent by the Company cleaning up & refitting	PILKHOUTE 1/10,000
	8th	9am	Training commenced on under Section Officers inspection	
		9.15 – 10.15am	Gun Drill	
		11.30 – 11.30am	Gas Drill	
		11.30 – 12.30pm	Bayonet Drill	
		1 – 3pm	Bomb throwing & rapid shipping	
			2nd Lieut. Wm MacIntyre is taken on the strength of Company & posted to No 1 Section	
	9th 10th 11th 12th 13th		Training carried on as above. The Company only attended church parade, no other work was carried out. Training as per attached Programme was carried out. Lt R.W. Yeldersbrough is taken on the strength of Company & posted to No 4 Section. Training as for 13th. Lt W.R. Kherard & 2/Lt T.K. Turner were taken on strength of coy & posted to Nos 2 & 3 Sections respectively.	
	14th		Training as for 14th. About 5pm an enemy High Velocity Shell struck the Officers mess. Killing 2 Lieut T.Y. Price & 2/Lt W.H. Thirlwell & wounding, Lt J.H Baxter, Lt W.R. Kherard, 2/Lt W. Williamson, 2/Lieut T. Turner, & Lieut W. Mac Intyre. Lt W.R. Kherard afterwards died of wounds.	
	15th			

WAR DIARY
or
INTELLIGENCE SUMMARY

Army Form C. 2118.

Place	Date	Hour	Summary of Events and Information	Remarks and references to Appendices
PIKEM	August 16th		The Company moved to "H" Camp. 2/Lt Crowder Boope was taken on the strength of the Company.	BIXSCHOOTE 1/10,000
	17th		The Company again moved. This time in the Caronin Farm Area, where the following Officers were taken on the strength of the Company as noted as shown	
	18th		Lt. E K Agnew — Transport Officer 2/Lt L V King } No 1 Section " JR Mellis Lieut C.F. Bruce } No 2 Section 2/Lieut S.F. Griffiths 2 Lieut A Stewart } No 3 Section 2 Lieut W A White } No 4 Section	
	19th	8 AM 8.15–9.15 am 9.15–10.150 am 10.30–11.30 am 11.30–12.30 pm 2–3 pm	Training for Coy again commenced Section Officers Inspection Gas Drill P.T. Gun Drill Blowing Guns Arm Drill	

			Remarks and references to Appendices
Place	Date	Hour	Summary of Events and Information	

Army Form C. 2118.

WAR DIARY or INTELLIGENCE SUMMARY
(Erase heading not required.)

Place	Date	Hour	Summary of Events and Information	Remarks and references to Appendices
PILKEM	August 20th 21st		Training of Company on the 19th " " " OC Coy Lt W.T. Adamson, 2 Lt J.R. Hamilton, 2 Lt V. King, and 5 K. Mills reconnoitred line MARSOUIN FARM – VILLA GRETCHEN with a view to choosing anti-aircraft positions to protect the artillery from low flying hostile aeroplanes.	BIXSCHOOTE 1/5,000
	22nd		2 Lt Priaulx, 2 Lt Hamilton, K. Mills, & Lt V. King received orders to proceed with a part of the machine gun [?] to prepare the positions. The company were recovering to relieve the 115th MG Coy in the Tuesday relieving 115 MGCoy approximately U 30 c 7.5.30 – c 30.1.5 which order to continue the S.O.S. cover of the infantry by putting a barrage down on a line approximately 500" in front of the Infantry front line positions. Sixteen guns were in position, the coy of the teams of 6 men, 1 sergt, 1 cpl per section. The Coy HQ PS were moved forward to NORMAN JUNCTION.	
	23rd 24th		Three days were spent in reconnoitring temporary shelter positions and generally improving their positions	
	25th		Orders were received to reconnoitre + find positions for 2 H guns in groups of 8 on the further side of the STEEN BEEK, with a view to providing a barrage for an attack by the 115th Bde	

WAR DIARY
or
INTELLIGENCE SUMMARY

Army Form C. 2118.

Place	Date	Hour	Summary of Events and Information	Remarks and references to Appendices
PILKEM	August 25th		The O.C. Coy reconnoitred & marked out positions & gave instructions for shell holes to be converted into gun emplacements on the evening of the 25th. Lieut Bruce & 2nd/Lieut R Hamilton, R.S.M King & 75 Gunners with 16 teams relieved the positions were dug by the teams relieved.	BIXSCHOOTE 1/10,000
	26th		In the evening the teams moved forward to their new positions & laid their guns on the new barrage line. Rain fell heavily & the ground soon became a morass & the gun positions full of water.	
	27th		The attack by the 115th Bde & the 116th Bde on the right commenced at 1.55 pm. The guns fired for 17 hours at the rate of 50 rounds per minute & then stood by ready to answer the S.O.S. by the Infantry. At 7pm the S.O.S. call was given & the guns put down their barrage intermittently for 2 hours. The enemy artillery showed much greater activity throughout the night than during the actual attack. Our casualties were 1 killed & 5 wounded. A few guns were specially situated to fire in groups of three on special targets from which intermittently throughout the night.	
	28th		A working party of 20 men came up to assist in making & forward dump of S.A.A. 12,000 rounds per gun were collected.	96

Army Form C. 2118.

WAR DIARY
or
INTELLIGENCE SUMMARY
(Erase heading not required.)

Place	Date	Hour	Summary of Events and Information	Remarks and references to Appendices
PILKEM	August 28th		The guns newly detailed on the 28th, again fired on the same targets throughout the night. There were 2 O.R. wounded during the night.	BUSCHOUTE 1/10,000
	29th		Pl: Goldsborough, 2/RWs Darby Stewart & Wheeler with teams, relieved the Officers & men in the line; 2/Lt Wheeler whilst at Coy at HUNNER JUNCTION. Preparations being made for a further attack by the Infantry & a new barrage line.	
	30th / 31st		On this case a return from 114 & 113 M.G. Coys are to be attached to this corps & the guns divided into groups of five. The barrage line is to be arranged so that they can enfilade the then line on any portion of the barrage line.	

Ronald Campbell M.Coy
O.C. 114 M.Coy

Confidential

Vol 7

War Diary

of the

176th Machine Gun Company

From 1-9-1917 to 30-9-1917.

(Vol.)

WAR DIARY
or
INTELLIGENCE SUMMARY

Army Form C. 2118.

Place	Date	Hour	Summary of Events and Information	Remarks and references to Appendices
	Sept. 1st		New barrage positions dug for 8 of the guns, which had been rather heavily shelled owing to their proximity to a trench tramway. These positions to a flank had to be very carefully camouflaged, owing to enemy aeroplanes, which flew over our positions very low every morning about 6 am.	Ref BIXSCHOOTE 1/10000
		2.40	2/Lts Griffith, King, and Nelles relieved officers and men in the barrage positions; ran into a slight barrage near the positions — 2 O.R. wounded.	
		3.0	1 Sergt. killed — 2 men wounded while relieved teams were on their way out. Lt. COOPE relieved CAPT. ADAMSON at NORMAN JUNCTION. Enemy aircraft very busy bombing at night.	
	4th		Positions dug in 1st inst. fairly heavily shelled - probably discovered by aeroplanes in early morning — 2 O.R. wounded.	
	5th		115 Machine Gun Coy. relieved us on night 5/6th in barrage positions. Fresh teams from ROUSSEL FARM (near H.Q.'s) under Lt. Potchborough 2/Lts. White, Stewart & Wheeler took over forward positions in the line from 113 and 114 Machine Gun Companies. Double relief carried out without a hitch. We had 12 guns in front defensive system, and 4 in reserve in the CANAL BANK.	
	6th		Usual aerial and artillery activity, though less shelling in new positions than in those we had left.	a.6.

2449 Wt. W14957/M90 750,000 1/16 J.B.C. & A. Forms/C.2118/12.

WAR DIARY
or
INTELLIGENCE SUMMARY
(Erase heading not required.)

Army Form C. 2118.

Place	Date	Hour	Summary of Events and Information	Remarks and references to Appendices
	Sept. 7th		2 4.2in guns in MILL withdrawn during bombardment of front line by "Heavies". Preparatory to sending out fighting patrols. Returned to positions at dusk.	Ref. LANGEMARK 1/10,000
	8th		Above operation repeated – similar result (NIL). This went further withdrawing from their exposed position the MILL under the observation of the Boche, was done in both occasions without any casualties.	
	9th		Another withdrawal as above for some reason – On returning after dusk after settling into position, men have pleasant surprise – find that 61st M.G. Coy has come to relieve them. Relief effected without incident. Rest of Bry got out all right – these 2 guns also after running into to separate barrages of H.E. & gas. Boche sent no parting souvenir, i.e. two from H.V. gun – no harm done.	Sheet 27 N.W.
	10th		Marched in afternoon from ROUSSEL FARM to ELVERDINGHE STATION.	
	11th		Bitter regrets on all sides at leaving such a healthy locality. Entrained at 3 p.m. – detrained INTERNATIONAL CORNER. Marched to STOKE FARM.	
EECKE	12th		Day spent in Interior Economy – soap issued – with good results. Foot-inspection preparatory to trek.	Ref. HAZEBROUCK 5a 1/100,000
MORBECQUE	13th		Started at 7:30 a.m. & arrived 11 a.m. at billets in EECKE area. Moved to billets in the MORBECQUE area.	

WAR DIARY
or
INTELLIGENCE SUMMARY
(Erase heading not required.)

Army Form C. 2118.

Place	Date	Hour	Summary of Events and Information	Remarks and references to Appendices
MORBECQUE	Sept. 14		Marched to ESTAIRES area.	Ref. HAZEBROUCK 5a 1/100000
ESTAIRES	15		Moved to RABOT FARM between STEENWERCK and PONT DE NIEPPE.	
RABOT FARM	16		The Company moved up to ARMENTIÈRES where it took over the duties of permanent nucleus garrison from 193 M.G. Coy. Here we met again 2/Lt. WHITE, and KING, who had been sent on in advance from MORBECQUE to take over, and who had remained here till the Company arrived. The relief was effected smoothly without any casualties.	
ARMENTIÈRES	17		The men were attached to the boy from the WELSH BATTALIONS were recalled to their Units and replaced on Keen mean to be transferred permanently to the M.G.C. 24 Guides were attached from the 115th Bde to act as guides to reinforcing Infantry.	FRANCE SHEET 36 N.W.
	18		Guides were busy reconnoitring Routes & Company engaged in reconnoitring S.O.S positions & dumps.	
	19		Do Do. There are approx. 53. M.G. emplacements in the defences of the town & therefore it takes some little time for the Enemy.	

2449 Wt. W14957/M90 750,000 1/16 J.B.C. & A. Forms/C.2118/12.

Army Form C. 2118.

WAR DIARY
or
INTELLIGENCE SUMMARY

(Erase heading not required.)

Instructions regarding War Diaries and Intelligence Summaries are contained in F. S. Regs., Part II. and the Staff Manual respectively. Title Pages will be prepared in manuscript.

Place	Date	Hour	Summary of Events and Information	Remarks and references to Appendices
ARMENTIERS	19		Teams to learn the various routes to them.	FRANCE SHEET 36 NW.
	20.		Received Instructions to reconnoitre & prepare a Barrage Scheme for 12 guns, the Barrage line to be from the River LYS at C17 a 3080 to STEP FARM at C17 & 20 40. LTS COOPE WHEELER & GRIFFITH reconnoitred the positions, and found that owing to the height of the BREWERY at C17 a 20 60, the Barrage line would have to be from RIVER LYS at C11 & 3520 to C17 & 3060. Company employed in opening up trenches & reconstructing emplacements.	
	21		The men are finding this part of the line a pleasant place with its comfort of huts & comfortable billets & pleasant employment on emplacements & trenches. Six guns are mounted against Aircraft & do night firing on appointed targets.	
	22 to 24		Employed on emplacements dumps & trenches. Each Section Making a quantity of approximately 12 positions each.	

2449 Wt. W14957/M90 750,000 1/16 J.B.C. & A. Forms/C.2118/12.

Army Form C. 2118.

WAR DIARY
or
INTELLIGENCE SUMMARY

(Erase heading not required.)

Instructions regarding War Diaries and Intelligence Summaries are contained in F.S. Regs., Part II. and the Staff Manual respectively. Title Pages will be prepared in manuscript.

Place	Date	Hour	Summary of Events and Information	Remarks and references to Appendices
ARMENTIERES	25		A further Barrage scheme required. LTS COOPE GRIFFITHS & WHITE reconnoitre positions — 12 Guns situated into 3 Groups of 4 to be able to put a Barrage of approx 500' on the enemy support line from I 5 d 4 3 14 to C 14 a 80 63.	FRANCE SHEET 36 N.W.
	26.		Scheme approved & Gun positions traced. CAPT W.L. ADAMSON returned from leave & resumed command.	
	27		Work commenced on Barrage positions.	
	28.		TRANSPORT commence rebuilding their stables under supervision of R.E.	
	29. 30.		Working on Barrage positions. Owing to the observation of low flying enemy aircraft all the work has to be done at night & carefully camouflaged.	

[signature]

Vol 8

Confidential

War Diary

of the

176th Machine Gun Company.

From 1.10.17 to 31.10.17.

(Vol.   )

Army Form C. 2118.

WAR DIARY
or
INTELLIGENCE SUMMARY
(Erase heading not required.)

Place	Date	Hour	Summary of Events and Information	Remarks and references to Appendices
ARMENTIERES	October 1st		Orders were received for a section of the Company to be held in readiness to proceed overseas on the 6th October. Preparations were immediately made to get this section complete in every detail as regards men, material and equipment. It was decided that 2/Lt. HAMILTON J.R. and 2/Lt. KING G.V. should accompany the section.	FRANCE SHEET 36 NW
	2nd to 5th		Work in Barrage line continued. Construction of emplacements, dugouts, ammunition recesses, pushed on with.	
	5		No. 2 Section, complete in every respect, left us for service overseas. Section 2 entrained at LA GORGUE for MARSEILLES.	
	6		Under a Divisional Scheme, the final of the R.F.A. Officers' Course attached to this Company arrived. This was a scheme whereby certain Officers from different batteries were attached for a week to Machine Gun Companies, and Officers from these Companies were attached to corresponding batteries. From 6th to 12th an Officer from B.122 was attached to this Company and an Officer from this Company to B.122.	illeg.

WAR DIARY or INTELLIGENCE SUMMARY

Army Form C. 2118.

Place	Date	Hour	Summary of Events and Information	Remarks and references to Appendices
ARMENTIERES	Oct. 7-13		Working continually on Barrage Positions. Tripods levelled and dug in, emplacements revetted, dugouts completed, trenches (which had formerly been drains) duckboarded, directors placed in emplacements. A great amount of camouflage was used, and work was often interfered with by low-flying hostile aeroplanes and also by balloons which were up early in the morning. On the 13th the teams of Nos. 4 Section which had been temporarily quartered in the BREWERY HOUPLINES moved into the dugouts constructed in barrage positions.	FRANCE SHEET 36.N.W
	14th	—	2 N.C.O's detailed for a course for N.C.O's of Machine Gun Companies in firing at low-flying hostile aeroplanes. This course is a highly necessary one, especially in this sector where there is an appreciable amount of such aerial activity. Lt. O. Cooke, 2nd in Command, left this day on transfer to 205th Machine Gun Company as additional Captain.	
	15th		The G.O.C. 115th Infantry Brigade inspected the Barrage position in detail and expressed himself as very well pleased with all the arrangements made as regards material, arrangement, and personnel. A practice test on S.O.S. line, which was	

WAR DIARY
or
INTELLIGENCE SUMMARY

Army Form C. 2118.

Place	Date	Hour	Summary of Events and Information	Remarks and references to Appendices
ARMENTIERES	Oct 15		Quite satisfactory.	FRANCE SHEET 36 NW
	16		Night firing was begun. One gun her section fires each night 1500 rounds. Targets were changed each night and also the different guns in each section were employed each night. It should have been mentioned that owing to the withdrawal of No. 2 Section, the Barrage Scheme has been slightly rearranged. There was now a 10 gun barrage; 2 of these guns did anti-aircraft work during the day from FARM POST and WEST WORKS and 2 more guns which has been withdrawn from the barrage line to ARMENTIERES to replace the 4 guns sent away on the 5th did the same kind of work.	
	17			
	18		Nothing of importance - usual work on barrage positions and night firing.	
	19		Officer from 376 Battery returned to his unit after a week's attachment to the Company.	
	20		Officer from B121 joined for week's attachment.	
	21		G.O.C. Division was to inspect the gun positions, but was unable to come and was represented by Lt. Col. Munby, G.S.O.I, who was quite satisfied with all arrangements.	
	22		Night firing as indicated on another basis by D.M.G.O who wished to systematize night firing throughout the Division. One gun per section	M.O.S.

Army Form C. 2118.

WAR DIARY
or
INTELLIGENCE SUMMARY

(Erase heading not required.)

Instructions regarding War Diaries and Intelligence Summaries are contained in F.S. Regs., Part II. and the Staff Manual respectively. Title Pages will be prepared in manuscript.

Place	Date	Hour	Summary of Events and Information	Remarks and references to Appendices
ARMENTIÈRES	22		was detailed on a permanent night firing gun. This gun's position and its zero line were very accurately fixed and transferred to a trench map. An arc was described at a radius of 1500° from the gun, showing the furthest limit at which the gun would fire; this arc was graduated on either side of zero in degrees and half-degrees. Lines were marked out showing the lowest range at which the gun could fire (1) When none of our patrols were out (2) When our patrols were out. A very varied selection of targets was supplied by the D.M.G.O. Thus different targets can be tackled each night. A list of targets proposed to be engaged is sent to Brigade at the beginning of each week, showing targets for that week. The first night's firing on the above lines - much easier and simpler than the previous way. Plates showing the exact area each gun can fire on were sent to B. M. G. O. and Brigade.	FRANCE SHEET 36 N.W.
	23			
	24		(2) Ground sheets supplied to cover tripods to protect them from the wet - a great improvement.	
	25		Six blankets fitted on dugouts and what is considered a patent night firing screen provided for the guns. This will appear in next month's technical report.	
	26		Officers of B/121 left after week's attachment. This attachment of Officers to Machine Gun Companies and vice-versa has been quite a success. Judging from the Officers who come to us, there is an astonishing	M.S.

2449 Wt. W14957/M90 750,000 1/16 J.B.C. & A. Forms/C.2118/12.

WAR DIARY
or
INTELLIGENCE SUMMARY
(Erase heading not required.)

Army Form C. 2118.

Place	Date	Hour	Summary of Events and Information	Remarks and references to Appendices
	Oct. 26		idea prevalent among what one might perhaps call the general public, that all that a machine gunner need do is to stick his gun up and fire into the void, quite insufficient as to whether the hits fired or provoked he makes plenty of noise. We are sanguine enough to hope that we corrected this erroneous impression. At any rate, both arms learnt to some extent, its powers and limitations of the other.	France Sheet 36 NW.
	27		Usual night firing tasks worthy on positions.	
	28.	At 9.30 p.m.	No. 1 Special Coy. R.E. fired gas bombs at 9.30 p.m. on enemy defences in C.29 a and part of C.29 b &c. We cooperated by firing on his original line. From ZERO to ZERO + 15 minutes at the rate of 100 rounds per minute. During the 15 minutes, the barrage lifted 200 x and then returned to its original line. From ZERO + 15 minutes to ZERO + 59 minutes, each gun fired 500 rounds intermittent on the same barrage line with a 200 x lift. Everything worked satisfactorily and the barrage was effective.	Ref. HOUPLINES 36.N.W.2 and N.E.1.
	29 -31		Work on ARMENTIERES DEFENCES and finishing off barrage positions.	

WOalshnoof Lieut.

Confidential

War Diary

of the

176th Machine Gun Company

from 1-11-1917 to 30-11-1917

(Vol.)

Army Form C. 2118.

WAR DIARY
or
INTELLIGENCE SUMMARY
(Erase heading not required.)

Instructions regarding War Diaries and Intelligence Summaries are contained in F. S. Regs., Part II. and the Staff Manual respectively. Title Pages will be prepared in manuscript.

Place	Date	Hour	Summary of Events and Information	Remarks and references to Appendices
ARMENTIERES	Nov. 1		Lieut. Agnew, transport officer left the Company and escorted sick.	
	2-4		Usual night firing programme continued.	
	5		New transport officer Lieut. Green joined the Coy from the Base	MAP REF. HOUPLINES 36 NW 2 & NE1 (Parts J)
	6		A registration of fire of the 4 guns of right Barrage Section was carried out Targets being in I 5 d. The actual attack of bullets on target could not be observed but direction was found to be accurate & ample safety clearance obtained over our outpost line. The object of this registration was to ascertain the effect of fire as regards direction & clearance with a view to future shoots.	
	7		Nothing of importance. Usual routine work.	
	8		At 1.24 am the 4 guns of right Barrage Section opened fire on what a road carried out G.L. SW 15 b. The targets selected & registered onto Coy formed the top side of a box barrage 100 on the flank of the hostility Pz.G. Fire commenced at the rate of 100 rounds per minute & was maintained for the firing 15 minutes after which rate was reduced to 1 belt per 9 minutes until	Gy

WAR DIARY or INTELLIGENCE SUMMARY

Army Form C. 2118.

Place	Date	Hour	Summary of Events and Information	Remarks and references to Appendices
ARMENTIÈRES	Nov 8		Zero + 2 hours after fire ceased. The operation as a whole was a complete success & reports indicate that the attached Gun Barrage was very effective. Nothing to report.	
	9		A one week programme of training was instituted for 16 O.R. in reserve.	
	10		Completing a system of relief for men on the line stated. The first batch of men drawn from the Barrage Sections commenced their week's training this day.	
	11		Work continued on emplacement & communications at Barrage positions also daily wiring parties carried on improving & repairing Team defences.	
	12		In response to S.O.S. call at 8:10 A.M. Barrage guns opened fire for a dal: period.	
	13		Visit of G.O.C. Division to Transport lines. Work in progress on stables & transport road under construction, was shown to him & met with general approval.	
	14		The D.M.G.O. made a tour of inspection of the Barrage positions at HOUPLINES during the morning.	
	15		Work on defences etc & casual night firing. Nothing unusual of importance to record.	

Army Form C. 2118.

WAR DIARY
or
INTELLIGENCE SUMMARY
(Erase heading not required.)

Instructions regarding War Diaries and Intelligence Summaries are contained in F. S. Regs., Part II. and the Staff Manual respectively. Title Pages will be prepared in manuscript.

Place	Date	Hour	Summary of Events and Information	Remarks and references to Appendices
ARMENTIÈRES	Nov 16.		Personal Letters received. His distinctive mark consists of a Red Stripe on black background & will now be worn on left sleeve by times of army all ranks of the Company.	
	17		G.O.C. Division visited the right and centre barrage positions. He was particularly pleased with the methods adopted and extent to which positions and approaches were camouflaged.	
	18		Usual routine.	
	19		Enemy placed a heavy barrage of H.E. near our gun emplacements fortunately without doing any material damage.	
	20		Usual routine.	
	21		The O.C. Coy. took over the duties of Commandant ARMENTIÈRES DEFENCES from Maj. Bingham who left on leave to U.K.	
	22-23		During these & preceding days much work was carried out on ARMENTIÈRES defences. Daily every parties were detailed to repair & strengthen its defences & also especially on the E & SE sides of the town.	
	24		At 5.0 a.m. in response to S.O.S. signal the barrage guns opened fire for a short period. C.S.M. Horley left the Coy. on his appointment to a regular commission in the Bedford Regt.	

WAR DIARY
or
INTELLIGENCE SUMMARY

Army Form C. 2118.

Place	Date	Hour	Summary of Events and Information	Remarks and references to Appendices
ARMENTIERES	Nov 24		A change over in the men training took place. It has been found that the system of relief is highly beneficial in various ways. Apart from the advantages of the M.G. training received and the return to private discipline the men derive great benefit from increased exercise, recreation and leisure.	
	25		Nothing of importance to record.	
	26		The 3 night Firing Guns were directed on to parts of enemy communication trench (MANS REDS) which during the day had been subjected to heavy destructive fire by our artillery.	MAP REF HOUPLINES 36 NW 3 & NE 1 (Photo 9)
	27-29		Owing to the weather, making of country + Takaka Zareka of the right Barrage system. An extensive drainage system has been found necessary. A large amount of time has been spent on constructive work in this connection.	
	30		The Brigadier General of the sector visited our centre Barrage Section.	

B.W. Marwin CAPT.
COMDG. 176 M. G. COMPANY.

Confidential

War Diary
of the
176th Machine Gun Company

1-12-1917 to 31-12-1917

(Vol)

WAR DIARY
or
INTELLIGENCE SUMMARY

(Erase heading not required.)

Army Form C. 2118.

Place	Date	Hour	Summary of Events and Information	Remarks and references to Appendices
ARMENTIERES	DEC. 1		The weekly change over of the men training took place	MAP REF. FRANCE 36 NW 1:40,000 HAZEBROUCK
	2 + 3		Nothing special to record. Usual wiring parties on the defences of the town and work improving barrage positions continued.	
	4		The barrage guns opened fire at 7.50 PM in response to SOS signal from our lines in the direction of FREZINGHEM.	
	5		The Machine Gun Company Commanders of the division held a conference under presidency of the D.M.G.O. at the H.Q. of 113 M.G. Company.	
	6		Capt. W.K. Adamson left the company to attend a Course at G.H.Q. Small Arms School, the command of the company being temporarily handed over to Lieut R.W. Goldsbrough.	
	7		The Commandant ARMENTIERES Defences returned from leave to U.K. and renewed his duties which during his absence had been performed by O.C. 176 M.G. Cy.	
	8		The men who had been training with the Yet Gee relieved a similar number of men on duty with the guns.	
	9		Pit Props supports were installed in all the cellar and dugout accommodation in use at Company H.Q.	
	10, 11 + 12		Nothing special to record.	

Army Form C. 2118.

WAR DIARY
or
INTELLIGENCE SUMMARY
(Erase heading not required.)

Instructions regarding War Diaries and Intelligence Summaries are contained in F.S. Regs., Part II. and the Staff Manual respectively. Title Pages will be prepared in manuscript.

Place	Date	Hour	Summary of Events and Information	Remarks and references to Appendices
ARMENTIÈRES	DEC 13		All the Lewis guns were laid on parallel zero lines with a good bearing of 90°. This alteration was made under orders of the DMGO with a view to simplifying fire control and facilitate rapid distribution or concentration of fire on to any target within range.	MAP REF: HOUPLINES 36 NW 2 & NE 1 (1 & 5) 1/10,000 FRANCE 36 NW 1/20,000
	14		The special working party, which had recently been assisting No. 1 Section in the construction of improved emplacements and extensive drawing operations, completed its task and was disbanded, the men joining their party opening their respective sections.	
	15		Weekly journal to report.	
	16		A special wiring party of 10 men was detailed for repair work on the defence wire defences East of N. HOUPLINES.	
	17			
	18		2nd Lieut Thiez departed on leave to UK.	
	19		The advance party of Australians made a reconnaissance of the position previous to taking over. The company was relieved by the 23rd Australian M.G. Coy. On completion of relief two orders proceeded to billets at H 19 & 10.05 to be in readiness to man and hold zero to the last the defences of FLEURBAIX in the event of enemy attack. The remaining section and H.Q. proceeded to billets near the transport lines at H 13 & 4.8.	
FORT ROMPU & FLEURBAIX	20			
	21 & 22		The two forward sections moved to billets at H 26 & 40 75. Reconnaissance of the defences of FLEURBAIX were made and men of the sections detailed to occupy the positions were conducted round.	
	23		A party of men from the section in reserve assisted in digging drains at the transport lines.	

WAR DIARY or INTELLIGENCE SUMMARY

Army Form C. 2118.

Place	Date	Hour	Summary of Events and Information	Remarks and references to Appendices
FORT ROMPU and FLEURBAIX	DEC. 24		Nothing to report.	MAP REF. FRANCE 36 N.W. 1/20,000
	25		Xmas Day. The Company was well outfitted with comforts thanks to the numerous funds of this kind in existence. These comforts were distributed in the morning and contributed towards making the festival as jovial as active service conditions permit.	
	26		Reserve dumps of S.A.A. for the defence of FLEURBAIX were established.	
	27		The twelve M.G. Guards who were left behind in ARMENTIÈRES when the Company was relieved rejoined the unit. The attached infantry who had been employed on similar duties rejoined their respective Battalions the day.	
	28		A fast "Stand to" for the garrison of FLEURBAIX was ordered at 5:30 am and was successfully carried out, all the stipulated M.G. positions being manned in quick time. Later in the day the two garrison sections moved to billets in the village.	
	29		Nothing special to report.	
	30		H.Q. and No. 3 Section moved forward to billets at H 26 & H 27.75 in readiness to take up supporting positions in the defence of HEUBAUX in case of attack.	
	31		Work done in improving sum biliard. The new recruit from England arrived complete with guns and limbers to take the place of the section which proceeded across from this company in October.	

COMDG. 176 M.G. COMPANY.

Confidential

Vol 11

War Diary

of the

176th Machine Gun Company.

From 1.1.1918 to 31.1.1918

(vol.)

WAR DIARY
or
INTELLIGENCE SUMMARY

Army Form C. 2118.

Place	Date	Hour	Summary of Events and Information	Remarks and references to Appendices
FLEURBAIX	Jan 1st (1916)		Under instruction from 38th Div. H.Q., a working party of 150 men was to be detailed to work round the FLEURBAIX DEFENCES under the supervision of O.C. 151st Field Coy. R.E. This party began work on this day. This left no men for training, which therefore had to be suspended temporarily.	Ref. FLEURBAIX trace.
	2nd		2/Lt. White W.A. rejoined the Company from B.E.F. Leave. Wind wiring party.	
	3rd		The new section sent from England to replace that ordered overseas on Oct 5th joined the Company at FLEURBAIX, billets having by this time been found for them.	
	4th		Capt. W.L. Cosens on rejoining the Company from course at CAMIERS. No wiring done as this was Sunday. The sections were reorganised, the new section being split up, individuals among the Company, it not being considered a good plan to work with a section entirely new to foreign service.	
	5th			
	6th		The D.T.U.F.O. visited the FLEURBAIX DEFENCES with O.C. Company, pointing out the position of the new concrete emplacements in process of construction by 151st Field Coy. R.E.	

WAR DIARY or INTELLIGENCE SUMMARY

Army Form C. 2118.

Place	Date	Hour	Summary of Events and Information	Remarks and references to Appendices
FLEURBAIX	Jan. 6th		The Detachment moved from BAC ST. MAUR to CROIX DU BAC (G.5 & 5.5.)	Ref. Sheet 36 FLEURBAIX 1/10000
	7th-9th		Nothing beyond usual wiring party. One section was carried on as the weather permitted for training, which was carried on as the weather permitted.	
	10th		Lt. Gen. Sir J.P. Du Cane KCB. Commanding XV Corps visited FLEURBAIX DEFENCES accompanied by G.S.O.2 Q.R.E., O.C. 151 Coy R.E. & O.C. 176 M.G. Coy. Everything apparently satisfactory.	
	11th		Capt. W.S. Ashmanson proceeded on leave.	
	12th		3 positions which were allotted two to country in case of attack in support of 114th Inf. Bde. were satisfactorily reconnoitred.	
	13th		O.C. 235th M.G. Coy. (12th Div. M.G. Coy.) accompanied by Brn. S.O. 17th Division, reconnoitred the FLEURBAIX DEFENCES preparatory to taking over.	
	14th		2/Lt. Stewart A. returned from B.S.T. leave.	
	15th		The Company was relieved in the FLEURBAIX DEFENCES by 235th Machine Gun Company. Relief carried out satisfactorily. On completion of relief, the Company moved billets in ESTAIRES.	
ESTAIRES	16th 17th –19th		Officers finally detailed to their respective Sections. As the M.G. Coy. billeted in ESTAIRES, this Company was responsible for occupying certain positions and bridgehead posts in case of	

WAR DIARY
or
INTELLIGENCE SUMMARY

Army Form C. 2118.

Place	Date	Hour	Summary of Events and Information	Remarks and references to Appendices
ESTAIRES	Jan. 17th–19th		attack on the Rotzyner. These positions were thoroughly reconnoitred by all the Officers of the Company and the majority of the N.C.O's and Mr. I.	Map Sheet 36a.
	20th		Church Parade – stafe reinforcement of 18 draft Lost 3 Sergeants supernumerary to establishment, joined the Company. A good training spirit having been obtained, a substitution must will throw training.	
	21st			
	22nd		2/Lr. Nellis H. proceeded on 8 days leave.	
	23rd–28th		Training proceeded with. Special attention paid to Barrage Drill, Lewis Drill, I.A., Elementary Advances Sun Drill, Passing of Orders Drill during long sustained firing and (last but not least) Physical Training and Recreational Training, the latter consisting of football mostly training.	
	28th		Lt. Company with Brigadier-General Commanding 115th Inf. Bde. and O.C. 113th Machine Gun Company proceeded by car to reconnoitre billets and tramps at ENGUINGATTE, whither the Company was shortly to proceed to do field firing.	
	29th		Usual training carried out. Capt. Wr. Adamson returning from leave.	

Army Form C. 2118.

WAR DIARY
or
INTELLIGENCE SUMMARY

(Erase heading not required.)

Instructions regarding War Diaries and Intelligence Summaries are contained in F. S. Regs., Part II. and the Staff Manual respectively. Title Pages will be prepared in manuscript.

Place	Date	Hour	Summary of Events and Information	Remarks and references to Appendices
ESTAIRES	Jan. 30th		Preparations for move and Interior Economy incidental to the move to ENGUINEGATTE.	Ref. Sket 36a. two
	31st		The Company started at 9 a.m. for ENGUINEGATTE. It was billetted for the night at GUARBECQUE.	

W/Washam J. Colt.
for O.C. 176th Machine Gun Company.

Confidential

WM 1²

War Diary
of
176th Machine Gun Company

From 1·2·1918   to 28·2·1918

(Ost.)

Army Form C. 2118.

WAR DIARY
or
INTELLIGENCE SUMMARY
(Erase heading not required.)

Place	Date	Hour	Summary of Events and Information	Remarks and references to Appendices
GUARBECQUE	Feb. 1st		The Company moved from GUARBECQUE to ENGUINEGATTE, where it was to be billeted for field firing. The Company was billeted in barns, which were fairly comfortable.	Sheet 3ba FRANCE 1/40000
ENGUINEGATTE	2nd		The day was spent in interior economy & settling down. The Company had baths at the mines at FLECHINELLE.	
	3rd		Sunday – in the morning cleaning of guns & tripods, spare parts and turning & cleaning of ammunition preparatory to firing. Training ground reconnoitred.	
	4th		This day was spent in firing the revolver course, after preliminary lectures and practice in snapping and trigger-pressing.	
	5th		Practices were carried out on the 25 yards range. Men were given practice in firing in Box Respirators and in coming into action quickly. A thorough practice in Barrage Drill was carried out, special steps being laid on. Points during long sustained firing and quick concentration and distribution. Problems were set on the ground.	
	6th		In the afternoon, a football competition on the 'knockout' principle was started.	
	7th		Firing a barrage practice with live S.A.A. which had been arranged for this day, had to be abandoned owing to rain, which came down continuously all day. Training carried on in billets.	

WAR DIARY
or
INTELLIGENCE SUMMARY

(Erase heading not required.)

Army Form C. 2118.

Place	Date	Hour	Summary of Events and Information	Remarks and references to Appendices
ENGINGHEM	Feb. 8th		Training had again to be confined to indoors work, owing to the bad weather. The D.M.G.O. came to stay here this day, and devoted the evening to lecturing the officers on recent developments in Machine Gunnery.	Ref. 36a France 1:20000
	9th		Barrage practice, with live S.A.A. was carried out on the field firing range. The following were practised:- (1) Concentration (2) Firing on an S.O.S. line (3) a surprise concentration. All were successfully carried out. In the afternoon the football competition was continued.	
	10th		Rain again spoiled a good programme of work, which had to be abandoned. The D.M.G.O. left for Division, having done much useful instructional work.	
	11th		Day spent in packing up and preparing to move.	
GUARBECQUE	12th		The Company moved to GUARBECQUE, where it billeted for the night.	Ref. Sheet 36 France & Belgium 1:20000
LA GORGUE AREA	13th		Moved to CHAPELLE DUVELLE.	
ARMENTIÈRES	14th		Moved to ARMENTIÈRES – H.Q. 78, RUE SADI CARNOT. Took over the following dispositions from 173rd Machine Gun Company (57th Division) 1 Section at TISSAGE - 1 Section at LILLE ROAD - 1 Section RUE FLEURIE Sector - 1 Section in reserve at LAUNDRY, midway between ARMENTIÈRES and ERQUINGHEM. Relief passed off without incident.	
	15th		Thorough reconnaissance of positions by O.C. Company. Some of the positions found to be of not much use, and others capable of improvement.	

Army Form C. 2118.

WAR DIARY
or
INTELLIGENCE SUMMARY

(Erase heading not required.)

Instructions regarding War Diaries and Intelligence Summaries are contained in F. S. Regs., Part II. and the Staff Manual respectively. Title Pages will be prepared in manuscript.

Place	Date	Hour	Summary of Events and Information	Remarks and references to Appendices
ARMENTIÈRES	Feb. 19th		Training programme made out and commenced for the section in reserve.	Ref. Sheet 36. FRANCE & BELGIUM 1/40,000
	17th 18th 19th		Training and work continued – trenches and emplacements improved. No. 4 Section relieved No. 1 Section at TISSAGE – the latter moved back to the LAUNDRY.	
	20th		Training and work as usual.	
	21st		Owing to a modification of the Divisional Defence Scheme, the section at the Laundry moved into the town to the École Professionelle. Orders received re the formation and establishment of the new Machine Gun Battalion. The 38th Bn. to be formed forthwith.	
	22nd		5 men returned from interviews preparatory to Transfer Tests.	
	23rd 24th		Work & training carried on as usual. No. 1 Section relieved No. 2 Section at LILLE ROAD – No. 2 moved to the ÉCOLE PROFESSIONELLE.	
	25th		Enemy raid in WEZ MACQUART section – some 6 our gun fired in their S.O.S. lines. 6 men were sent down by 17th R.W.F., and 6 men by 10th S.W.B.	
	26th		to complete the new establishment required by the new Battalion organisation. A programme of work was made out and	

Army Form C. 2118.

WAR DIARY
or
INTELLIGENCE SUMMARY
(Erase heading not required.)

Instructions regarding War Diaries and Intelligence Summaries are contained in F. S. Regs., Part II. and the Staff Manual respectively. Title Pages will be prepared in manuscript.

Place	Date	Hour	Summary of Events and Information	Remarks and references to Appendices
ARMENTIÈRES	Feb. 26 Cont?		begun - not less than 3 hours per day being devoted to Mechanism and Gun Drill.	Ref. Sheet 36 FRANCE & BELGIUM 1/100,000
	27th		N.C.O. detailed for a course in firing at low-flying aeroplanes at GOSNAY.	
	28th		Usual work and training.	

Wilson Smith ? Capt.
for O.C. 176 M.G. Coy.